Mathematical Minds

A Guide to Assessing Attainment Target One

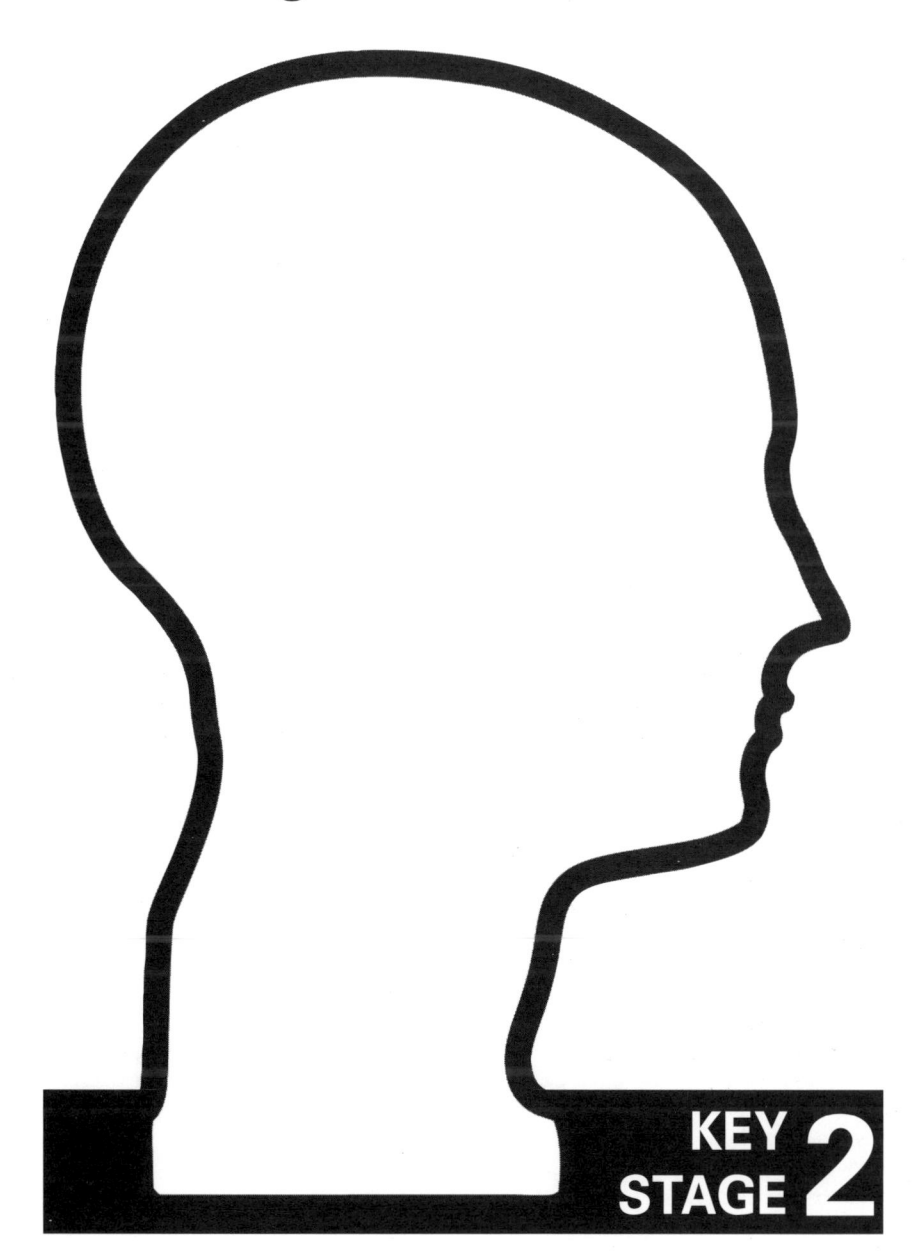

KEY STAGE 2

Hanna Vappula
National Foundation for Educational Research

Published by nferNelson Publishing Company Ltd
The Chiswick Centre
414 Chiswick High Road
London W4 5TF, UK

www.nfer-nelson.co.uk

nferNelson is a division of Granada Learning Limited, part of Granada plc.

© NFER-NELSON, 2003

All curriculum references are taken from:
Department for Education and Employment and Qualifications and Curriculum Authority (1999) *The National Curriculum for England: Key Stages 1–4*. London: HMSO.

All rights reserved, including translation. Except where otherwise indicated, no part of this publication may be reproduced or transmitted in any form or by any means, electronic or mechanical, including photocopying, recording or duplication in any information storage and retrieval system, without permission in writing from the publishers and may not be photocopied or otherwise reproduced even within the terms of any licence granted by the Copyright Licensing Agency.

Photocopying restrictions
Photocopying restrictions will be waived on certain pages within this publication, indicated by the inclusion of this symbol, on full payment of the invoice accompanying it. This is intended to aid you in the effective use of the materials within your organisation. Until full payment is received, all photocopying restrictions remain in force and any photocopying is illegal.

Once the book has been purchased, please note that:

a) All other copyright restrictions remain in force.
b) Photocopies may only be made for use *within* the purchaser's school, department or other organisation. Photocopies may not be made for distribution to other organisations. In particular, the waiving of photocopying restrictions does *not* cover this book's use in surveys or large-scale research projects.

If you have any doubts about your use of the photocopiable material in this book, please telephone nferNelson and ask for the Contracts Manager.

Typesetting by Oxford Designers & Illustrators
Printed by Thanet Press, Margate, Kent

Code 0090008638   ISBN 0 7087 0369 0   1(02.03)

Contents

Acknowledgements v

Introduction 1

Exploring number 2

Measuring 6

Paper folding 10

Plan a holiday.. 14

Shape game 20

Mathematics levels for Attainment target 1... 25

Acknowledgements

We would like to thank all the schools that gave us permission to try out these activities, and all the teachers and pupils in these schools who took part in the activities and provided samples of work.

(Please note that the spelling and grammar in the examples of pupils' work has not been corrected.)

Introduction

This book describes techniques that can help you assess pupils' performance in Attainment Target 1 (AT1). After you have used the activities in this book, you should find that you are able to see opportunities for assessing AT1 during other class activities, with little or no adaptation of tasks or interruption of learning.

Each section of this book:
- describes an activity;
- links to the National Curriculum Programme of Study (e.g. Ma2/1f);
- gives guidance on how to assess pupils' performance;
- discusses samples of pupils' work.

The aim is to give you ideas about how assessment of AT1 can be carried out in class during activities that are useful and interesting for pupils, and to help you use the results of assessment to further develop pupils' skills.

In some cases, you may choose to assess one pupil or a small group by observing them while they work and by asking questions, while at other times you may wish to assess the whole class by, for example, asking them to produce a written record that can be marked.

When using the activities in this book, the following points should be borne in mind:

- Assessment objectives are given for each activity. These summarise the areas in which pupils will have opportunities to demonstrate their skills. However, you will not necessarily either want or be able to assess all these areas in the course of one activity. You may choose to focus on one in particular if you are assessing a large number of pupils or, if assessing an individual or a small group, you may be able to use observation and questioning to assess a wider range of skills.

- The nature of the skills being assessed means that you need to step back from what pupils are doing and allow them to solve their own problems and come to their own conclusions as much as possible. If you find that you have to give help and support, try prompting the pupil to solve the problem first. You will need to take into account during assessment the amount of support needed, since the ability to work independently, think for oneself and work out solutions is an important aspect of AT1.

- In some cases, pupils need to have particular subject knowledge to be able to successfully complete an activity. If you want to focus on assessment of AT1, you will need to be sure that the activity is within the scope of what pupils have previously learnt. Otherwise, pupils may not be able to demonstrate the specific skills which you want to assess. Remember that your aim is not to assess knowledge or understanding in other areas, only in AT1.

- General guidance is given about the levels of attainment that can be identified for the samples of pupil performance in each activity. This does not necessarily imply that the pupil is definitely at this level – rather that this particular observation or piece of work can be judged to be evidence of work at this level. To build up a definite judgment of a pupil's level in AT1, you would need to gather evidence from a wider range of work.

- For convenience, the levels for AT1 are described on page 25.

Activity

Exploring number

MATHEMATICAL CONTEXT

Ma2 Number
- Recognising and describing number patterns, recognising their patterns and using these to make predictions; making general statements, using words to describe a functional relationship, and testing these (Ma2/2e).

ASSESSMENT OBJECTIVES

During this task, you may be able to observe whether the pupils can:

Problem solving
- find different ways of approaching a problem in order to overcome any difficulties (Ma2/1d);

Communicating
- organise work and refine ways of recording (Ma2/1f);
- present and interpret solutions in the context of the problem (Ma2/1h);

Reasoning
- understand and investigate general statements (Ma2/1j);
- search for pattern in their results; develop logical thinking and explain their reasoning (Ma2/1k).

Materials needed
- Number cards from 4 to 10
- Plenty of counters in two different colours – at least four of each colour for each pupil
- Paper for writing down observations

A brief outline

The pupils are going to explore number sequences. They will identify the number of odd and even numbers in each pattern and explain the reasons for their findings.

The activity

1 Introduce the task

Tell the pupils that they are going to explore odd and even numbers. Remind them of what these are.

Show a set of number cards from 4 to 10. Ask how many cards there are altogether, how many odd numbers, and how many even numbers. Acknowledge that there is one more even than odd number. Write on the board: '4, 5, 6, 7, 8, 9, 10 – one more even than odd', then show the same situation with counters:

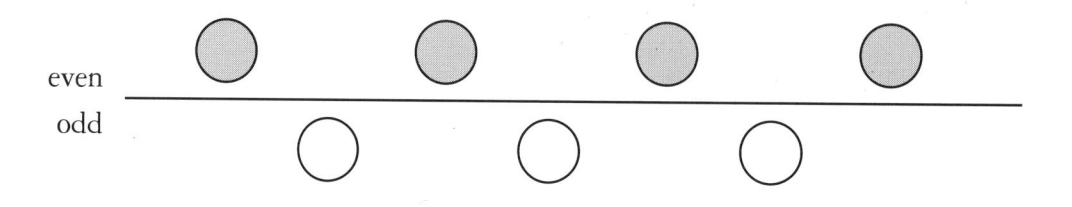

Then ask the pupils what would happen if the cards were numbered from 4 to 12. Prompt the pupils if necessary to say that there would still be one more even than odd number. Write on the board: '4, 5, 6, 7, 8, 9, 10, 11, 12 – one more even than odd'.

Ask what would happen if there were cards from 2 to 12, and again confirm the answer. Write on the board: '2–12 – one more even than odd'.

2 Work through the task

- The pupils should now work individually or in pairs. They should have plenty of counters and a piece of paper to write down their observations. Encourage the pupils to focus on choosing the starting and finishing numbers and describing the relationship between the numbers of even and odd.

- The pupils are likely to work at different paces, so you may wish to write the following instructions on the board.

    a) Find out what other possibilities there are with consecutive number sequences than to have one more even than odd number. You can choose your starting and finishing numbers.

    b) Then explore sequences where every second number is kept (e.g. 4, 6, 8, …).

    c) Next explore sequences where every third number is kept.

    d) Then explore sequences where every fourth number is kept.

    e) Finally, can you see a pattern in your results? Try keeping every fifth, sixth, seventh number etc., if you have not yet noticed a pattern.

- Encourage the pupils to choose their own ways of working and presenting their results. Some pupils may wish to work solely with counters and present their conclusions in drawings. Others may find it easier to write down number sequences and circle the relevant numbers in each case.

Guidance on assessment and examples of pupils' work

(a) and (c) – consecutive numbers and every third number kept

Look for evidence that the pupil has recognised that there are three possible relationships of odd and even numbers – equal numbers, one more odd number, one more even number. They should observe that there are equal numbers of odd and even numbers when the starting number is odd and the finishing number even, or vice versa. There is one more odd number when both the starting and the finishing numbers are odd. There is one more even number when both the starting and the finishing numbers are even.

(b) and (d) – every second and every fourth number kept

Pupils draw the conclusion that all the numbers in the sequence are either odd or even.

(e) – overall conclusions

Keeping every nth number – if n is odd you will have three possible relationships of odd and even numbers; if n is even you will have either all odd or all even numbers.

Exploring number

Example 1: Jake

Jake started off by exploring different sequences of ten numbers. He came to the conclusion that half of the numbers were odd and half were even.

2, 3, 4, 5, 6, 7, 8, 9, 10, 11.
Odd: 5
Even: 5

3, 4, 5, 6, 7, 8, 9, 10, 11, 12.
Odd: 5
Even: 5

1, 2, 3, 4, 5, 6, 7, 8, 9, 10.
Odd: 5
Even: 5

He said that he had done the task and the answer was 'five'. Jake was asked if there were any other possibilities of odd and even numbers than five of each. At first Jake said 'no'. He was advised to try some other numbers to see if that really were the case. This time Jake decided to explore sequences of six numbers. Again, he found that there were an equal amount of odd and even numbers.

4, 5, 6, 7, 8, 9.
Odd: 3
Even: 3

3, 4, 5, 6, 7, 8.
Odd: 3
Even: 3

5, 6, 7, 8, 9, 10.
Odd: 3
Even: 3

Jake read on the board that the pupils were asked to draw conclusions from their results. He suggested that, with sequences of ten and six numbers, you can halve the total number and that will tell you how many odd numbers there are and how many even numbers there are.

If you have 10 numbers it will half it so it will be 5. If you have 6 numbers half it again and then it will be 3.
10 numbers = 5
6 numbers = 3

At this point Jake was prompted to try keeping every second number. He was shown with counters how to do that. However, Jake was not confident enough to progress into the following parts of the task.

Jake presented his work in a clear and organised way. He showed some evidence of Level 3 performance in this aspect of his work. However, Jake's problem-solving skills sometimes seemed to be holding him back. For example, he failed to try different approaches to overcome difficulties in solving the task. He chose the numbers ten and six at random. This strategy might have led him to find different types of consecutive number sequences. However, Jake did not recognise the importance of both 10 and 6 being even numbers. In this sense, he failed to identify information necessary for solving the task fully.

Jake's problem-solving skills were of a Level 2 standard in this task. He attempted

Mathematical Minds Key Stage 2

to draw conclusions from his results, and his performance showed evidence of beginning to discuss his mathematical work and explain his thinking. However, this did not happen completely spontaneously. Indeed, Jake seemed to be searching for a single-word answer (e.g. 'five') and started drawing more elaborate conclusions only after receiving external support. In order to progress from Level 2 to Level 3 in AT1, Jake would need to demonstrate more spontaneous and detailed thinking skills when solving problems.

Example 2: Gita

Gita was able to provide examples of consecutive number sequences where there is one extra odd number, and where there is one extra even number. She started formulating rules for her findings. However, she did not realise the role of the last number in her number sequences. This hindered her from formulating complete and correct conclusions from her results.

9, 10, 11, 12, 13, 14, 15,   odd, 4   even, 3

8, 9, 10, 11, 12, 13, 14,   even, 4   odd, 3

if you start with a odd number you get more then even.
And if you start with a even number you get more then an odd number.

Gita worked with counters and also recorded some of her observations. When she explored keeping every second number, she wrote down numbers from 1 to 10. She then circled every second number. At this point her work led her to conclude that there were as many odd as even numbers. Although this was an incorrect conclusion, it indicated that she could have reached a more valid result if she had continued to work with counters and had not been distracted by the need to record her work in writing.

1, ②, 3, ④, 5, ⑥, 7, ⑧, 9, ⑩   even, 5   odd, 5

When you start with every 2rd number up in 10s you will get the same answers.

Gita then explored keeping every third number. She noticed an alternating pattern of odd and even numbers. However, she expressed this rather clumsily. Also, she failed to make a link with her findings in the first part.

1, 2,③,4, 5,⑥,7, 8,⑨,10, 11, ⑫, 13, 14, ⑮

if you start with every 3rd number you get a odd number and a even number togher.

Finally, Gita explored keeping every fourth number. She interpreted her example, correctly concluding that all numbers were even. However, Gita only explored one number sequence, thus failing to note that sometimes taking every fourth number would result in all numbers being odd.

1, 2, 3,④,5, 6, 7,⑧,9, 10, 11, ⑫, 13, 14, 15, ⑯, 17, 18, 19, ⑳   All even

Gita organised her work and checked her results, which was evidence of work at Level 3. In order to demonstrate attainment at Level 4, Gita would have needed to check more systematically that she had covered all relevant cases. Her problem-solving skills in this task were comfortably within Level 3. She seemed to have a good idea of what type of an answer she was looking for and also used different approaches to overcome difficulties in solving different parts of the task. However, Gita had not grasped all the key information necessary for solving the task fully. Her reasoning skills showed strength in understanding the basic requirements of the task, but her weakness seemed to be in trying to find a pattern in her results. Overall, Gita worked comfortably within Level 3 in AT1 for this task.

Activity

Measuring

MATHEMATICAL CONTEXT

Ma3 Shape, space and measures
- Converting between centimetres and millimetres or metres, explaining methods and reasoning (Ma3/4a).
- Using suitable measuring instruments for a task (Ma3/4b).

Ma4 Handling data
- Representing and interpreting discrete data using graphs and diagrams, including bar charts (Ma4/2c).
- Drawing conclusions from statistics and graphs (Ma4/2f).

ASSESSMENT OBJECTIVES

During this task, you may be able to observe whether the pupils can:

Problem solving
- recognise the need for standard units of measurement (Ma3/1a);
- identify the data necessary to solve a given problem (Ma4/1c);
- select and use appropriate calculation skills to solve problems involving data (Ma4/1d);

Communicating
- decide how best to organise and present findings (Ma4/1f);

Reasoning
- explain and justify their methods and reasoning (Ma4/1h).

Materials needed
- Measuring tape
- Two small pieces of paper for each pupil
- Calculators

A brief outline
The pupils will use their paces (steps) to estimate a distance and present their results in bar charts. This task is best carried out with a group of five or six pupils.

The activity

1 Introduce the task

Introduce the idea of measuring a distance when it is not practical to use a measuring tape. Choose a distance that you are going to use for the task (e.g. the width of the classroom or the edge of the playground).

2 Work through the task

- Each pupil writes their name on their two pieces of paper.
- Each pupil walks the route and counts the number of steps they take. They write this on one of their pieces of paper.

Mathematical Minds Key Stage 2

- Collect this information from all the pupils. Ask the pupils to arrange the pieces of paper from the smallest number to the largest number. Draw a bar chart with the bars increasing in size.
- Next, each pupil will measure the length of their step using a measuring tape. They write their result on their second piece of paper.
- Collect this information from all the pupils. Ask the pupils to arrange the pieces of paper from the largest number to the smallest number. Draw a bar chart with the bars decreasing in size.
- Ask the pupils how they would calculate an estimate of the distance using the two pieces of information they have collected. Each pupil uses their two figures to calculate their estimate. Draw a bar chart showing these results.
- Compare the results presented in the three bar charts. Discuss reasons behind any similarities in the charts. For example, in the first two charts the names may have remained almost in the same order. If there are no such similarities, lead the discussion into exploring why this might surprise you.

Guidance on assessment and examples of pupils' work

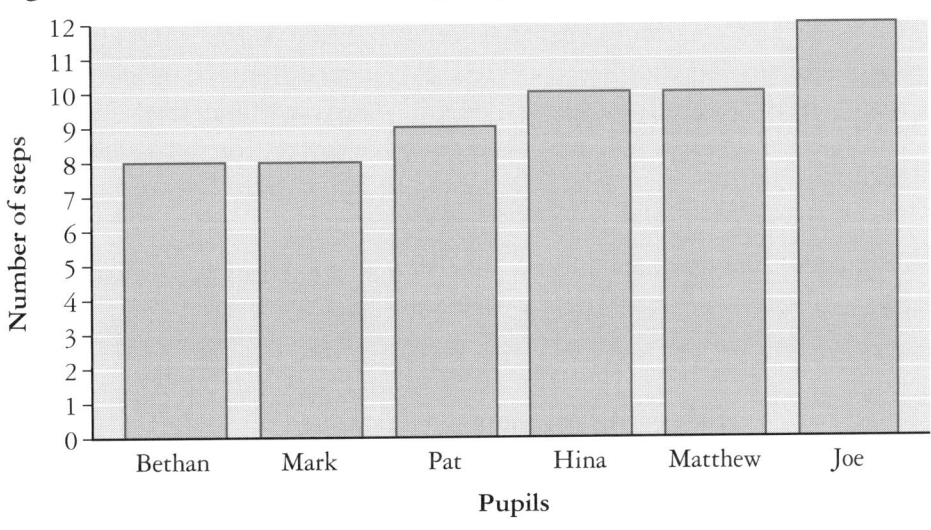

Figure 1: First bar chart showing steps taken

Figure 2: Second bar chart showing length of step

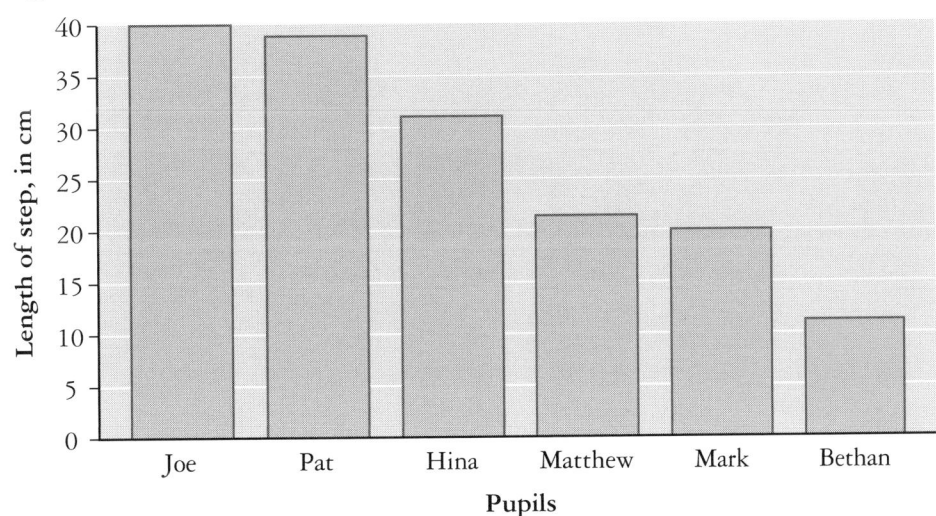

Joe often tried to take an active role in solving the task, only to realise that he had misunderstood the instructions. For example, when the first pieces of paper had been collected, Joe tried to convince other members of his group that they should be put in the order in which the pupils had walked the route. He eventually gave in and the bar chart was drawn as in Figure 1.

In the next stage, Joe wanted to measure the whole distance with the measuring tape. At this point, the instruction to measure one step *only* was repeated. Some pupils started measuring their steps by standing still while another pupil carried out the measuring. They realised that they should either use centimetres or inches so that they could compare one another's results. Joe considered the task at hand. He then announced that he was going to walk to the point where the measurement was taken so that he knew his step would be the right length. He took care with this task making sure that his gait was natural. Joe was also very concerned that the pupil measuring his step would read the scale correctly. The pupils in this group measured their step from the toe of their back shoe to the heel of their front shoe. None of the pupils in this group realised that they had skipped one shoe length in their measurements. The group discussed how the scale of the bar chart should be constructed when the results varied from 12cm to 40cm. They decided to write in every fifth value. Joe did not take part in this discussion or the drawing of the bar chart showing length of step (see Figure 2).

The group was asked how they would calculate an estimation of the distance using the two pieces of information they had collected. Joe seemed thoughtful when he listened to other pupils' suggestions. Finally, he said that you would need to multiply them together. He was able to elaborate on his suggestion by using his own pair of results as an example: *'because there are 12 lots of 40. It's 40 centimetres, then another 40 centimetres, then another 40 centimetres, 12 times. So it's 12 times 40.'*

Each pupil calculated their estimate and the results were shown in a third bar chart (see Figure 3).

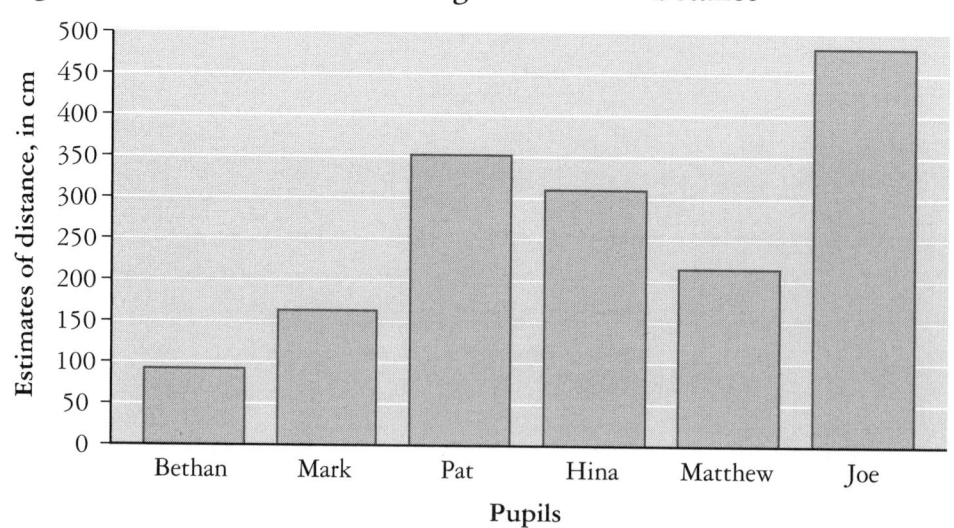

Figure 3: Third bar chart showing estimates of distance

All three bar charts were put on the wall. The group was asked to look at them and compare them. They were asked to discuss the results. First, the pupils examined the last bar chart which showed the estimated distance. They felt confident that the two lowest bars could not be accurate. One pupil said: *'If I lie down on the floor I can't get from that end to that end, and I'm definitely taller than 96 cm!'*. Joe did not show evidence of being able to interpret the information presented in the bar charts.

The group was next advised to compare the first two bar charts and say if there were anything that surprised them. They were prompted to think about the relationship between the number of steps taken and the length of a step. The pupils could not immediately draw a link between these two factors. They were prompted further by asking whether someone who takes many steps has long or short steps. Joe said instantly that the person would have short steps. The rest of the group seemed slightly hesitant but Joe was very sure about his idea. He jumped up and demonstrated how someone taking very short steps would need to take more of them, whereas someone taking very long steps would only need a few to get from one end to the other. The group still found it difficult to understand that the bar chart surprisingly did not show this. For example, from the chart it appears that Joe took many long steps, and Bethan took fewer, shorter ones.

In several instances, Joe showed competence in using his problem-solving and reasoning skills. When posed with a question, Joe often seemed to stop and think. On the other hand, he sometimes had difficulties listening to the given instructions. He also showed less confidence in presenting and interpreting information in bar charts. In this task, Joe's AT1 communication skills were below the demands of the task. However, he showed his understanding of the situation by describing it mathematically, and he gave an explanation of his reasoning. This indicates that he is beginning to work at Level 5 in AT1, although his ability to use and apply mathematics would benefit from the development of a more robust understanding of common ways of presenting data.

Activity

Paper folding

MATHEMATICAL CONTEXT

Ma3 Shape, space and measures
- Visualising and describing 2-D and 3-D shapes and the way they behave, making more precise use of geometrical language, especially that of triangles and quadrilaterals (Ma3/2b).
- Making and drawing with increasing accuracy 2-D and 3-D shapes and patterns (Ma3/2c).

ASSESSMENT OBJECTIVES

During this task, you may be able to observe whether the pupils can:

Problem solving
- approach spatial problems flexibly, including trying alternative approaches to overcome difficulties (Ma3/1c);

Communicating
- organise work and record or represent it in a variety of ways when presenting solutions to geometrical problems (Ma3/1d);

Reasoning
- use mathematical reasoning to explain features of shape and space (Ma3/1h).

Materials needed
- Two A4 sheets of paper for each pupil or pair
- One sheet of sugar paper for each pupil or pair
- Glue
- Scissors

A brief outline
Pupils will investigate different methods of folding rectangular pieces of paper to make squares.

The activity

1 Introduce the task

Discuss the properties of a square. Remind the class that all sides of a square are the same length. Show how halving a square will give two right-angled triangles.

Tell the class that you want to fold an A4 sheet of paper so that you end up with two squares that are the same size, and are the biggest possible that you can get from that sheet of paper. Introduce the following paper-folding method to the class.

Fold the paper in half, so that the fold is parallel to the shorter side.

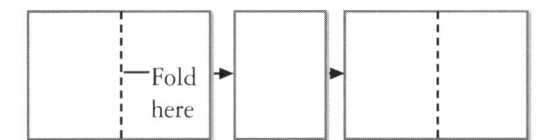

Fold two corners on one of the long sides so that they touch the middle fold, then fold the top part over.

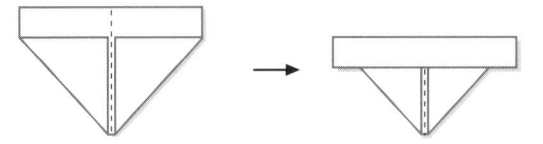

Open it up. You can now cut out two squares that are the same size and are the biggest possible.

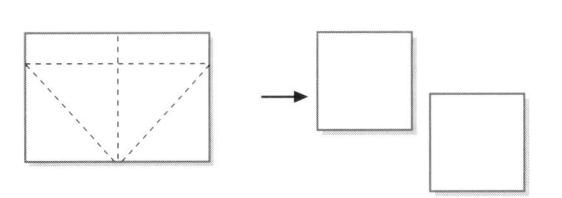

Display these different stages of folding the paper on the wall so that pupils can see them while they are working on the task.

Ask the pupils to find rectangular pieces of paper for which the method works, and those for which it does not work. Their aim should be to come up with a rule of the sizes of the rectangles for which the method works or does not work. Stress that you want to cut out two squares that are the same size and are as big as possible.

2 Work through the task

- Pupils work individually or in pairs.
- They find out whether the paper-folding method introduced to them will work with *all* rectangular pieces of paper. They need to use their A4 sheets of paper first to make rectangles of different sizes. Then they experiment to discover if the method always works.
- When the pupils find rectangles that cannot be folded by the method described above, they should try to come up with a rule that defines when the method works and when it does not work.
- Pupils then try to find alternative methods that can be used with rectangles on which the original method cannot be applied.
- Pupils present their findings in a poster.

Guidance on assessment and examples of pupils' work

The method works if $a \geq \frac{1}{2}b$.

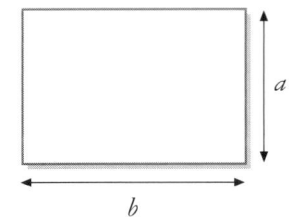

Example 1: Lauren

Lauren attempted to solve the problem through estimating by eye only. She did not feel comfortable about folding the paper even when prompted. Lauren's inflexibility in trying out different problem-solving strategies led her to conclude incorrectly that the paper-folding method could not be applied to the bottom shape in her poster.

Paper folding

I think this shape will work because it is a Decent size to work with.

I think this shape won't work Because it is small and even if it did do the folds it would Be uneven.

Lauren's work in this activity could not achieve Level 2 in AT1 as she was unwilling to explore the mathematical context effectively.

Example 2: Connor

Connor started by cutting squares from his A4 sheets of paper. He tried different sized squares and recognised that the method worked each time. This finding was something Connor thought would be interesting to put in his poster.

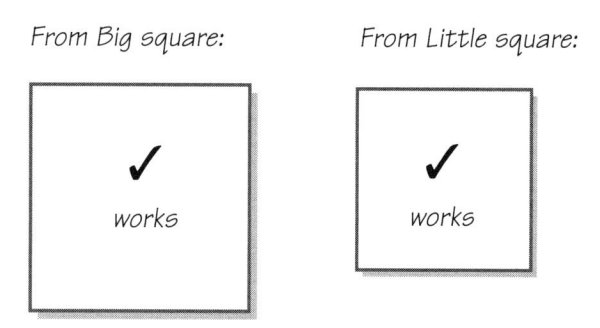

From Big square: *From Little square:*

✓ works

✓ works

Connor recognised that the shape of the original piece of paper mattered rather than its size. However, he did not know how to present this information in his poster. While he was thinking about it, another pupil had found that the method did not work with long and thin rectangles. Connor immediately took this on board and wrote it in his poster with an appropriate example.

This method works on big and small squares.
But doesn't work on Long, thin rectangles.
Long thin rectangle: Does not work.

✗ Doesn't work.

Connor successfully drew conclusions from the properties of some shapes. He was capable of providing particular examples of cases that followed a rule, although he did not systematically try to find out if all rectangles followed his rule. He was also generally quite hesitant in his approach to drawing conclusions. Connor showed evidence of Level 3 reasoning skills.

Example 3: Alex

Alex presented his solutions clearly. He attached folded pieces of paper on his poster with arrows pointing to the relevant features.

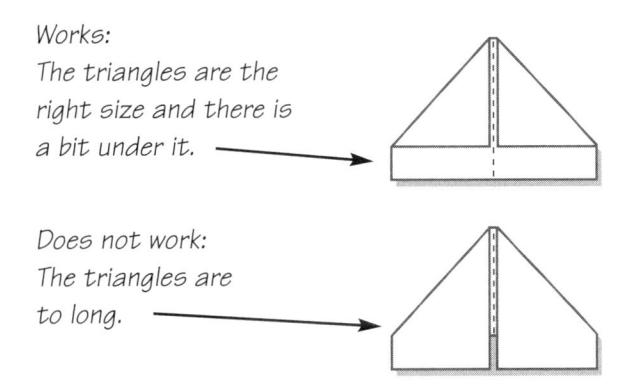

Works:
The triangles are the right size and there is a bit under it.

Does not work:
The triangles are to long.

Alex showed a Level 4 standard of reasoning skills in actively searching for a geometrical feature that would lead him closer to the overall solution. However, he struggled with generalising from his findings. His problem-solving skills were comfortably within Level 3 in AT1.

Example 4: Molly

Molly discovered quickly that the given method would not work when the rectangle was long and thin. She then focused on finding an alternative method, and found two new paper-folding methods for cases when the original method did not work. On her poster Molly attached folded pieces of paper and explained her results in a step-by-step manner.

But if you cut the ends off look:

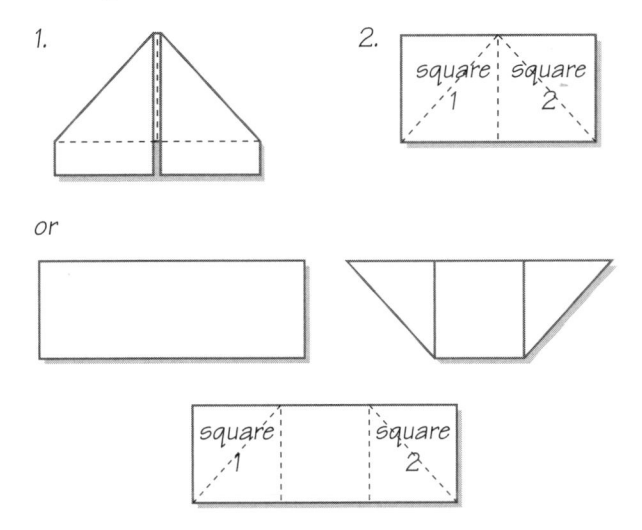

1.

2. square 1 | square 2

or

square 1 | square 2

Molly's poster relied heavily on visual cues. However, at the end of the lesson she was able to explain her work verbally to the class. She did this with confidence and her description was unambiguous.

Molly's problem-solving skills in this task were of Level 5 standard in AT1. She worked completely independently and showed considerable enthusiasm for the task. She drew simple conclusions of her own and gave an explanation of her reasoning. However, Molly did not attempt to find out how long and thin the rectangles had to be for the original paper-folding method to be ineffective, despite being prompted to do this.

Paper folding

Activity

Plan a holiday

MATHEMATICAL CONTEXT

Ma4 Handling data
- Solving problems involving data (Ma4/2a).
- Interpreting tables, lists and charts used in everyday life (Ma4/2b).

Ma2 Number
- Choosing, using and combining any of the four number operations to solve word problems involving numbers in 'real life' (money) (Ma2/4a).
- Using a calculator for calculations involving several digits, including decimals (Ma2/3k).
- Knowing how to enter and interpret money calculations (Ma2/3k).

ASSESSMENT OBJECTIVES

During this task, you may be able to observe whether the pupils can:

Problem solving
- approach problems flexibly, including trying alternative approaches to overcome any difficulties (Ma4/1b);
- identify the data necessary to solve a given problem (Ma4/1c);
- select and use appropriate calculation skills to solve problems involving data (Ma4/1d);

Communicating
- decide how best to organise and present findings (Ma4/1f);

Reasoning
- explain and justify their methods and reasoning (Ma4/1h).

Materials needed
- Calculators for each individual or pair
- Paper to write down working
- Two handouts per individual or pair (Handout 1: Flights and trains, page 18; Handout 2: Hotels, page 19)

A brief outline
Pupils use flight information, train timetables and hotel prices to plan a holiday within given restrictions.

The activity

1 Introduce the task
Explain to the class that the Cooper family are going on holiday to Italy. First they will fly to Rome, but will not stay the night there. From the airport they will travel to one of four smaller towns where they will spend all their holiday. They have £1500 to spend on flight tickets, on connecting train journeys between Rome and their final destination, and on hotels.

The pupils are going to help the Coopers plan their holiday. They will need to make sure that the family do not overspend. They will also need to make sure that the flight timetables and train timetables do not clash.

All prices are for the whole family. Some of the prices are in pounds and some are in euros.

2 Work through the task

- Pupils work individually or in pairs.
- They need calculators and paper to write down their ideas. Give out the two handouts with information about prices and timetables.
- Encourage the pupils to show their reasoning, even if they later decide to solve the task differently.

Guidance on assessment and examples of pupils' work

While the pupils are completing the task, observe their use of problem-solving strategies. Ask them to explain why they have made particular decisions. Look for evidence of acknowledging the different types of information presented in the handouts, leading to a recognition of the different options available. One efficient approach is to start with the information readily available, i.e. the timetables. All prices can be initially scanned through. Currency conversions are not necessary until the pupils reach the final stage of checking whether they have solved the task within the given limits. However, some preliminary conversions may be useful in giving an idea of the magnitude of the prices. Pupils should recognise that they need to select prices that are as low as possible. They should also notice that differences in hotel prices outweigh the effects of differences in train ticket prices on the total cost. Observe pupils' strategies if they find that their approach leads to a dead-end. The best way forward would be to learn from the situation and try another approach.

The table below lists total prices for all travel options in pounds. Shading indicates an insoluble clash between flight times and train times. You may find this table a helpful resource when checking pupils' work. The correct answer is to buy a ticket costing £743.80 and stay in Bari for 3 nights.

Flights	6 nights			3 nights		
	£733.30	£610.80	£782.10	£743.80	£736.70	£1081.20
Destinations						
Siena	£2536.49	£2413.99	£2585.29	£1696.49	£1689.39	£2033.89
Assisi	£2902.52	£2780.02	£2951.32	£1873.52	£1866.42	£2210.92
Ancona	£2191.62	£2069.12	£2240.42	£1540.62	£1533.52	£1878.02
Bari	£1905.10	£1782.60	£1953.90	£1443.10	£1436.00	£1780.50

Example 1: Daniel

Daniel started with the cheapest flight. He worked out how much money he had left after buying the flight tickets. He also wrote down the times of travelling from London and arriving in Rome. Next he chose train tickets to the destination that had the cheapest train tickets, i.e. Assisi. He started writing down the amount of money spent and the times of travelling. He then realised there would not be enough money to select this travel option so abandoned the cheapest flight. Next he

Plan a holiday

worked through each flight ticket as presented in the table and insisted on travelling to Assisi. Eventually, there was only one flight ticket left to try. Daniel thought that this was the correct option. He started to work neatly on the other side of his paper. However, once again Daniel insisted on travelling to Assisi. By now, he had stopped writing down anything and continued working out the cost using his calculator. Finally, he made a note that he had run out of money.

Daniel tried different flight tickets when his first solution failed, but he did not vary the destination. Thus he showed some organisation in his work, but his problem-solving strategies were limited. The evidence indicated that he was working at Level 3 in AT1 for this task.

Example 2: Georgia

Georgia started solving the problem by converting the total amount of money into euros. She then converted all four hotel prices into pounds. Although most prices were in euros, Georgia continued to work in pounds for the rest of the question.

£1500 = 2380.95EUR
Siena = £283.50
Anaconda = £220.50
Assisi = £346.50
Bari = £157.50

Georgia chose the cheapest flight and wrote down all the key information. She then chose the destination that had the cheapest hotel price, i.e. Bari. Georgia carried out the correct calculations for the total cost of the journey. She concluded that this was the correct answer.

Flight £610.80 = 6 nights
Train = Bari = £226.80
6 nights in Bari = £945.00
total = £1782.60

Georgia sensibly based her initial choice on the cheapest flight ticket and cheapest hotel price. She showed evidence of paying attention to relevant information when she wrote down the prices for each hotel. She also realised that, with her choice of flight ticket, the family would spend six nights in the destination. However, Georgia had ignored fundamental information by overlooking the financial constraints. Like Daniel's, her work was of Level 3 standard in AT1.

Example 3: Sanjay

Sanjay started off by looking at the different types of information given in the handouts. He did not write anything down for a while. He was looking at flight information for flying back when he realised that this could be a good starting point. He noticed that one of the flight times was different from all the others. Sanjay worked his way through all the train ticket information trying to find a train ticket that would bring the Coopers back in time for the early morning return flight. Failing to find such a train he concluded that the Coopers could not take this flight at all. He crossed the flight out in the table. Next, Sanjay worked his way through the times of flights from London to Rome. He wrote the name of each destination for which a connection could be caught. Sanjay realised that he could not take the £782.10 flight because there were no connecting trains. He had now crossed out two flight tickets, and realised that the Coopers could not go to Siena.

£733.30	Ancona, Assisi, Bari
£610.80	Ancona, Assisi, Bari
~~£782.10~~	
£743.80	Assisi, Bari
~~£736.70~~	
£1081.20	Assisi, Bari

Next, Sanjay decided to work out one of the travel options that were still available. He selected the cheapest flight ticket and picked the first destination in his list, Ancona. After making the appropriate calculations he concluded that there was not enough money to select this travel option.

107.40EUR
350EUR × 6
107.40EUR
= 2314.80EUR
= £1458.32

£1458.32 + £610.80 = £2069.12

Sanjay realised he needed to select an option which required staying fewer nights. This time he chose Bari because it had the lowest hotel price.

180EUR
250EUR × 3
180EUR
= 1110EUR
= £699.30

£699.30 + £743.80 = £1443.10
travelling to Bari, £56.90 left

Sanjay focused effectively on identifying the necessary information before attempting to find a solution to the problem. He showed his understanding of the situation when he eliminated some options before attempting any calculations. The evidence from this activity indicates that Sanjay was working at Level 5 in AT1.

Pupil handout 1

Flights and trains

£1500 to spend on flights, train tickets and hotel

Flight tickets

Return ticket for the whole family	Number of nights	Flying away day	leaves London	arrives in Rome	Flying back day	leaves Rome	arrives in London
£733.30	6	Mon	10:30	14:00	Sun	18:00	19:40
£610.80	6	Mon	07:40	13:05	Sun	18:00	19:40
£782.10	6	Mon	16:05	21:25	Sun	18:00	19:40
£743.80	3	Thu	13:45	17:15	Sun	18:00	19:40
£736.70	3	Thu	11:00	16:05	Sun	09:25	13:00
£1081.20	3	Thu	11:00	16:05	Sun	18:00	19:40

Train tickets to four towns – Siena, Ancona, Assisi and Bari

Rome to Siena
08:47 → 11:31
11:45 → 15:20
price one-way 81,10 EUR for the whole family

Rome to Ancona
14:14 → 18:07
15:37 → 18:45
price one-way 107,40 EUR for the whole family

Siena to Rome
10:15 → 13:37
14:50 → 18:16
price one-way 81,10 EUR for the whole family

Ancona to Rome
11:15 → 14:23
15:15 → 18:23
price one-way 107,40 EUR for the whole family

Rome to Assisi
15:37 → 17:19
20:41 → 23:33
price one-way 71,60 EUR for the whole family

Rome to Bari
10:27 → 17:00
18:38 → 23:32
price one-way 180,00 EUR for the whole family

Assisi to Rome
12:24 → 14:23
16:30 → 18:23
price one-way 71,60 EUR for the whole family

Bari to Rome
07:43 → 12:22
13:43 → 18:22
price one-way 180,00 EUR for the whole family

1 euro = £0.63

Hotels

Siena Hotel

Family Price:
450 EUR/night

ANCONA HOTEL

Family Price:
350 EUR/night

Assisi Hotel

Family Price:
550 EUR/night

BARI HOTEL

Family Price:
250 EUR/night

1 euro = £0.63

Activity

Shape game

MATHEMATICAL CONTEXT

Ma3 Shape, space and measures
- Visualising and describing 2-D and 3-D shapes and the way they behave, making more precise use of geometrical language (Ma3/2b).
- Making 3-D shapes with increasing accuracy (Ma3/2c).
- Visualising and predicting the position of a shape following a rotation, reflection or translation (Ma3/3b).

ASSESSMENT OBJECTIVES

During this task, you may be able to observe whether the pupils can:

Problem solving
- approach spatial problems flexibly, including trying alternative approaches to overcome difficulties (Ma3/1c);

Communicating
- organise work and record or represent it in a variety of ways when presenting solutions to geometrical problems (Ma3/1e);

Reasoning
- use mathematical reasoning to explain features of shape and space (Ma3/1h).

Materials needed
- Plenty of multi-link cubes
- Three sheets of A4 paper for each group
- Three ready-made shapes for each group (using pictures given on page 24)
- Screens or other dividers to provide privacy for each group, or some other method of preventing them from seeing each other's shapes

A brief outline
The pupils use mathematical terminology to instruct fellow pupils to construct shapes using multi-link cubes. This activity can be carried out as a game if wished.

The activity

1 Introduce the task

Remind the class of the three key dimensions of a cuboid. Use the multi-link cubes to show examples of cuboids with different dimensions. Make sure that the pupils know how to describe a cuboid (e.g. 4 by 6 by 2) and how to work out the total number of cubes (e.g. 48 cubes altogether).

Discuss different ways of building a shape. Show the pupils an L-shaped construction using 12 cubes. Ask them how they would instruct someone who can not see it to build it. Explain that you might start by making two 3 by 2 by 1 cuboids and then linking them together. Point out that the instructions about linking them together would have to be very clear. Alternatively, you could start

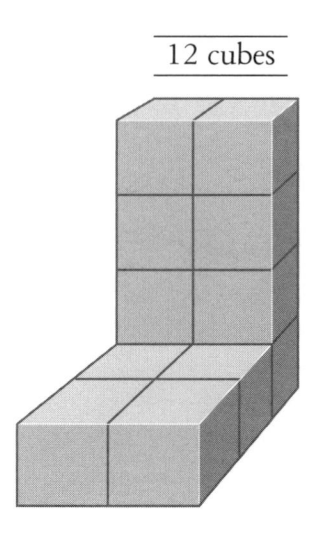

12 cubes

Mathematical Minds Key Stage 2

with a 4 by 3 by 2 cuboid and take off a 3 by 2 by 2 cuboid from one corner. Demonstrate these examples using the multi-link cubes.

Discuss different ways of making the instructions easy to follow – for example, start with a statement of the number of cubes needed altogether and use numbering or bullet points to separate each step.

2 Work through the task

- Pupils work in groups of three.

- Each group needs a working area that cannot be seen by other groups. Each group needs plenty of multi-link cubes to work with. There should also be three ready-made shapes for which the group will write the instructions. Pictures of the shapes are given on page 24. Half of the class should be given the shapes in the left-hand column, and half of them should receive those in the right-hand column.

- The groups discuss the shapes and write their instructions. This may take about 45 minutes. Groups that work fast could write up several instructions for each shape, including observations of the advantages of some instructions over others. Alternatively, they could make their own shapes and write instructions for building them.

- All shapes are dismantled and the class comes together. Each group will have a chance to read out at least one set of instructions for one of their shapes. Departures from their written instructions are allowed. Simultaneously, a group who has not seen the shape will try to build it while the rest of the class watches. If the shape is constructed successfully, the instructors will get one point in the game. You may also give points to other groups if they can come up with alternative instructions that are at least equally as good.

- Go through each shape one at a time.

- Finally, you can add up the points for each group.

Extending the task

All the sets of instructions could be compiled into a folder to make an activity booklet for other pupils to use. Ask the pupils to choose the best instructions for each shape, and feed this information back to those who wrote the instructions. You may wish to add new shapes to the folder. Ask the pupils to build any shape they like and write instructions for it. This may help pupils to recognise features of shapes that are easy to describe.

Guidance on assessment and examples of pupils' work

Look for evidence that the pupils use spatial methods flexibly. This can be observed when the pupils choose the quickest strategies for building the shapes. It can also be seen in their ability to view their own instructions from another person's perspective.

Look for effective use of mathematical vocabulary in the pupils' interactions.

Example 1: Tristan (and his group)

6 cubes

You will need 8 cubes.
1. *make a sqare with 4 at the top and the bottom*
2. *take two from the corner*
3. *twist the left in the middle*
   til the cube lookes like
4. *twist it 180°*

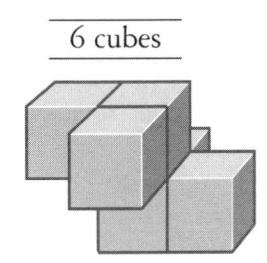

Initially the first step on Tristan's instructions read: *'You will need . . . cubes'*. He left a blank space for the number of cubes needed, because he wanted to see which method of constructing the shape would be the clearest to explain. This shows evidence of planning in advance. After Tristan had completed his instructions, he was reminded that he had not written the number of cubes. He wrote '8'. When asked if it should say 6 instead, he confidently defended the 8, explaining that he had started with a cube, made up of 8 multi-link cubes.

In steps 3 and 4, Tristan was struggling with the task of rotating the top part of his shape. He decided that drawing a picture might be a good way of expressing his thoughts, although this did not really fit the aim of the activity. Then he decided to use the degrees as a measure of turn to help him.

You will need 18 cubes.
1. *make a cube (2 by 3)*
2. *take the top bit off of it*
3. *leave four cubes on each corner*
4. *now you leave the top 9 and check if it has 13 cubes all together*
5. *now you will have a tableshape cube*

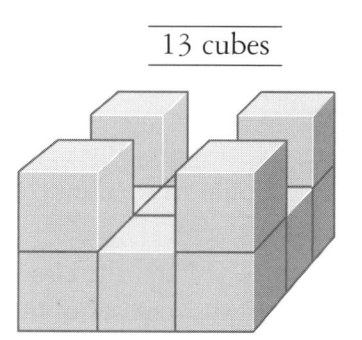

13 cubes

In explaining his second shape, Tristan showed that he has understood the importance of checking work (step 4). In step 5, Tristan described the shape as *'table-shaped'*. This showed that Tristan was confidently developing his own ideas when solving shape problems. However, he needs to do more work on expressing himself using correct mathematical language (e.g. step 1).

Tristan's working showed evidence of approaching spatial problems flexibly. He started from a larger cuboid and worked through the task by removing cubes. In this case, however, Tristan's approach was more complicated than necessary. He would benefit from supportive guidance on using his spatial skills more effectively. Tristan used degrees and drew a diagram to describe the rotation of part of the shape, thus overcoming a difficulty when solving the problem. He also showed evidence of checking his work and explaining his thinking. However, his instructions were not clear enough to enable other pupils to make the shapes he described. Tristan showed evidence of working at Level 3 in AT1 for this activity.

Duncan found a shorter approach to describe Tristan's second shape.

You will need 13 cubes.
- *Put 9 cubes together on one shape of a square.*
- *Put 1 cube on each corner.*
- *There you have your shape.*

13 cubes

Duncan's instructions were clearer than Tristan's, and more accurate and concise. They were still not wholly sufficient as the corner cubes could be misplaced, but the evidence indicates that he could be working at Level 4 in AT1.

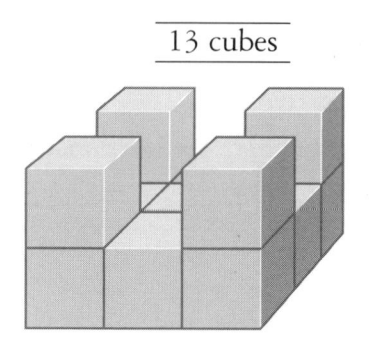

Mathematical Minds Key Stage 2

Example 2: Leah (and her group)

Shape 1
1. Collect twenty cubes.
2. Make a 3 by 4 cube base.
3. Make a 2 by 3 top part.
4. Add two cubes either side of the second/middle row of the 2 by 3 top part.
5. Connect the longest column on the top part to the middle column on the base.
6. You then have your shape.

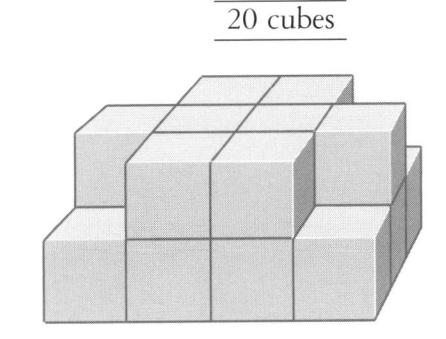

20 cubes

In step 4, Leah used a feature of the shape in order to communicate her ideas efficiently. She was particularly pleased with this line in her instructions. After successfully instructing another group to build the shape, Leah explained to the class that the second/middle row could only be on the longer side of her shape. She said that the shorter side only had two rows, neither of which could have been the middle row.

Some of Leah's instructions were unclear and wordy. However, Leah showed good problem-solving skills in recognising these weaknesses and adapting her instructions according to the audience. She realised that the fifth step in her instructions needed clarification regarding the point at which the shapes were to be connected. Leah read this line as: *'Connect the longest column on the top part to the middle column on the base, so that the flat sides are together'.*

Shape 2
1. Collect 23 cubes.
2. Make a 3 by 4 rectangle.
3. Make a 3 by 3 square.
4. Add 2 connected cubes to 1 side of the square.
5. On the same side as you connected the two extra cubes, connect the 3 by 4 rectangle.
6. Your shape is finished.

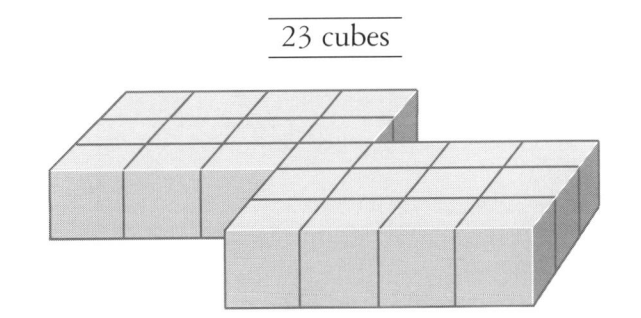

23 cubes

Leah seemed worried as she was approaching step 5. This time she was unable to come up with an improvement to her instructions. However, being able to identify the most difficult parts in her instructions showed some evidence of being capable of checking her work. While Leah was reading out the instructions, one pupil in her group whispered that steps 2 and 3 should refer to cuboids, rather than a rectangle and a square. Leah did not follow this advice. She would benefit from consolidating her vocabulary of 2-D and 3-D shapes.

For these two shapes Leah's group chose a way of building the shapes that was longer than necessary. In both cases they could have started with a bigger shape and proceeded by removing cubes. The instructions given by the pupils were ambiguous. Leah's work in this task showed evidence of achievement at Level 3, but was not sufficiently clear and organised to reach Level 4 in AT1.

Shape game

Resource sheet

Shapes to get ready for the groups

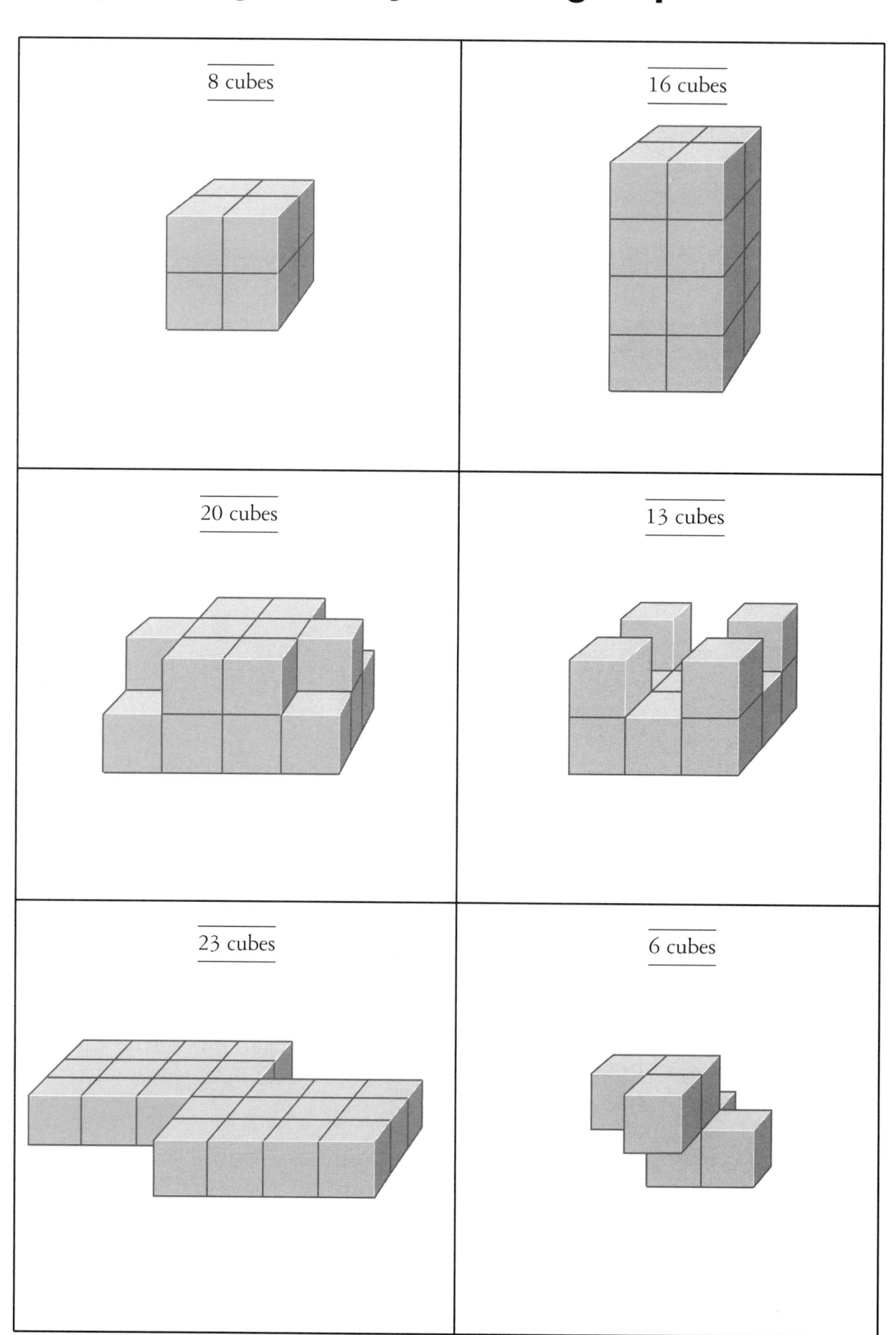

8 cubes

16 cubes

20 cubes

13 cubes

23 cubes

6 cubes

© NFER-NELSON, 2003. All rights reserved. This sheet is part of *Mathematical Minds KS2*, ISBN 07087 0369 0 and may be photocopied.
Published by nferNelson Publishing Company Ltd, The Chiswick Centre, 414 Chiswick High Road, London W4 5TF, UK.
nferNelson is a division of Granada Learning Limited, part of Granada plc.

Mathematics levels

Attainment target 1: Using and applying mathematics

Teachers should expect attainment at a given level in this attainment target to be demonstrated through activities in which the mathematics from the other attainment targets is at, or very close to, the same level.

Level 1

Pupils use mathematics as an integral part of classroom activities. They represent their work with objects or pictures and discuss it. They recognise and use a simple pattern or relationship.

Level 2

Pupils select the mathematics they use in some classroom activities. They discuss their work using mathematical language and are beginning to represent it using symbols and simple diagrams. They explain why an answer is correct.

Level 3

Pupils try different approaches and find ways of overcoming difficulties that arise when they are solving problems. They are beginning to organise their work and check results. Pupils discuss their mathematical work and are beginning to explain their thinking. They use and interpret mathematical symbols and diagrams. Pupils show that they understand a general statement by finding particular examples that match it.

Level 4

Pupils are developing their own strategies for solving problems and are using these strategies both in working within mathematics and in applying mathematics to practical contexts. They present information and results in a clear and organised way. They search for a solution by trying out ideas of their own.

Level 5

In order to carry through tasks and solve mathematical problems, pupils identify and obtain necessary information. They check their results, considering whether these are sensible. Pupils show understanding of situations by describing them mathematically using symbols, words and diagrams. They draw simple conclusions of their own and give an explanation of their reasoning.

Level 6

Pupils carry through substantial tasks and solve quite complex problems by independently breaking them down into smaller, more manageable tasks. They interpret, discuss and synthesise information presented in a variety of mathematical forms. Pupils' writing explains and informs their use of diagrams. Pupils are beginning to give mathematical justifications.

Level 7

Starting from problems or contexts that have been presented to them, pupils progressively refine or extend the mathematics used to generate fuller solutions. They give a reason for their choice of mathematical presentation, explaining features they have selected. Pupils justify their generalisations, arguments or solutions, showing some insight into the mathematical structure of the problem. They appreciate the difference between mathematical explanation and experimental evidence.

Level 8

Pupils develop and follow alternative approaches. They reflect on their own lines of enquiry when exploring mathematical tasks; in doing so they introduce and use a range of mathematical techniques. Pupils convey mathematical or statistical meaning through precise and consistent use of symbols that is sustained throughout the work. They examine generalisations or solutions reached in an activity, commenting constructively on the reasoning and logic or the process employed, or the results obtained, and make further progress in the activity as a result.

Exceptional performance

Pupils give reasons for the choices they make when investigating within mathematics itself or when using mathematics to analyse tasks; these reasons explain why particular lines of enquiry or procedures are followed and others rejected. Pupils apply the mathematics they know in familiar and unfamiliar contexts. Pupils use mathematical language and symbols effectively in presenting a convincing reasoned argument. Their reports include mathematical justifications, explaining their solutions to problems involving a number of features or variables.

Department for Education and Employment and Qualifications Authority (1999) *The National Curriculum for England: Key Stages 1–4.* London: HMSO.